OUR MINISTRY, HIS WORDS

"The Continuation"

By: Anelda L. Ballard

Co-author Jean A. Scott

Romans 15:5-6 (NKJ)

Now may the God of patience and comfort grant you to be like-minded toward one another, according to Christ Jesus, that you may with one mind and one mouth glorify the God and Father of our Lord Jesus Christ.

Our Ministry, His Words
"The Continuation"

By: Anelda L. Ballard
Co-author: Jean A. Scott

Cover designed by: Anelda L. Ballard
Logo designed by: Andre M. Saunders
Editor: Anelda L. Ballard
Photography by: John "Rolex" Kollock of Philadelphia, PA,
www.photobucket.com, www.istockphoto.com and www.fotosearch.com
Hair Stylist: Roxanne Meade

© 2009 Anelda L. Ballard

ISBN 978-0-9768540-1-2
ISBN 0-9768540-1-5

All rights reserved. This book is protected under the copyright laws of the United States of America. This book may not be copied or reprinted for commercial gain or profit. The use of short quotations or occasional page copying for personal or group study is permitted and encouraged. Permission will be granted upon request. Scripture quotations are from the King James Version, New King James Version, New International Version and the New Living Translation of the Holy Bible.

For Worldwide Distribution. Printed in the United States of America
Published by Jazzy Kitty Greetings Marketing & Publishing, LLC
Utilizing Microsoft Publishing, Adobe, and Book Cover Pro Software

ACKNOWLEDGMENTS

I like to thank God because without Him, His Son Jesus Christ and the Holy Spirit, I could not have done this. I like to thank my husband Ronald Ballard Jr. for his love, continual prayers and constant support. I want to thank my daughter MoNae L. Lewis, my father Cleveland Scott Jr. and my mother Jean A. Scott who is also the co-author of this book.

I want to thank all of my family, friends and my authors. A special thank you to Larenda, Sharnika, Marquita, Myria, Nadine, Lil Bo, Jaden, Tymir, my God children RJ and Kaprice. Thank you to my dear friends; Anthony Gaddy, Mark Flowers, Tony Crawford, Rob Young, Regina, Nita and Wendi. Thanks to my proofreaders; Alisha, Faith, Molly and Joe Ashe. Thank you Pastor Donia Gonzales-Copeland, Pastor Janice of Women Regaining Strength, Shabach Productions, the support of Rose Davis of Lula Enterprises, Jessie's II Boutique, 1260 AM Radio Broadcast, Ingram Book Group and Lightning Source.

Thank you to Senior Pastor David Pope and First Lady Terri Pope of New Life Christian Center, who helped in elevating my poetry and spiritual gifts. You both helped me give God my very best. Also, having me perform with Clifton Davis was an honor and God Gets the Glory!

To Pastor Ethelynn Taylor (my second mom). This book is also in memory of my friend, The Late Harold Taylor "Herbie" and my sister-in-law The Late Tanya James. I miss you both and I will always love you.

A special thanks to Leona Dorsey, after your book *Be Encouraged* was given to me, I have been inspired to finish what God started. Your book has the right name, *Be Encouraged!* I will continue to pray for you daily.

I pray that you are encouraged by the poetry. Most importantly, know that it was inspired by God. My mother and I love you, God Bless you all.

DEDICATIONS

We dedicate this book back to God and His Son Jesus Christ who is our Savior and Leona Dorsey a very special Women of God, who was also healed by God. She is an inspiration to us.

Also my husband Ronald and my daughter MoNae thank you for your patience, understanding, support and love. That's why this book is dedicated to the both of you, I love you! Kitten

To my husband Cleveland Scott Jr., you have been very supportive and loving through all of this, therefore I dedicate my portion of this book to you. Especially the poem "Count Your Blessings" that I wrote in our first book because I do "Count My Blessings" everyday I think of you. Your loving wife Jean. I also wrote the poem "Help Me Fill My Fathers Shoes" in memory of my father, The Late Arthur Glover. I miss you dad, your daughter Jean.

OUR MINISTRY, HIS WORDS

Introduction..	Page i
Our Prayer..	Page 02
Help Me God Fill My Fathers Shoes............................	Page 04
On The Outside Looking In..	Page 07
You Are The One I Choose..	Page 09
I Will Not Procrastinate Again.....................................	Page 11
Ecclesiastes 3:1-8 (A Time for Everything).................	Page 13
Keep Your Head Up...	Page 14
Suffering Through Hurt or Pain...................................	Page 15
Celebrate Your Special Love.......................................	Page 17
We All Need To Give Love...	Page 18
God Can Forgive The Adulterer...................................	Page 19
You Will See Your Husband Again...............................	Page 20
I Should Be Dead...	Page 22
My Secret...	Page 25
Passage Psalm 63:1-8...	Page 27
Cover Me Lord!...	Page 28
Keep Christ In Christmas...	Page 31
Pick Your Weeds..	Page 32
Serenity Prayer...	Page 33
A Victim of 9/11..	Page 34
Pick Up Your Bed And Walk...	Page 37
Another Woman You Call Wife.....................................	Page 39
Attempt of Suicide..	Page 41
A Mother With An Urgent Prayer..................................	Page 45
Peace and Love Within..	Page 47

OUR MINISTRY, HIS WORDS

Your Tears Are Only Temporary	Page 49
My Life Is In Your Hands	Page 51
I Believe God	Page 53
In Heaven All-Day	Page 54
I Wait For The Key To Turn	Page 57
God Released My Spiritual Gifts	Page 60
Find My Daddy Who Looks Just Like Me	Page 63
God's Will	Page 64
God Doesn't Make Mistakes	Page 67
He Will Never Abandon You	Page 71
Will You Change?	Page 73
What About Me?	Page 74
The Lord's Prayer (Psalm 23)	Page 76
I Have A Testimony	Page 78
Preparing For Baptism	Page 81
Using Music To Get Through	Page 85
I am Somebody Too	Page 86
Tsunami/Hurricane Katrina	Page 88
I Can't Forget	Page 90
Jesus Is My Friend	Page 92
The Invitation	Page 94
Where Are You Going?	Page 95
Inspirational Scriptures	Page 96
Closing Prayer	Page 103
Assignment Complete	Page 104

INTRODUCTION

This book is the continuation of Poetry is Our Ministry "to Touch the Heart." God has blessed my mother and I with the spiritual gift of writing poetry. Through our lifetime, we both had experiences like most people that God had to cover us and He was the only one that we could depend on to get us through the roughest times of our life. That's when my mother and I found poetry.

As we stated in our first Introduction in Poetry is Our Ministry "to Touch the Heart," our only true purpose for writing these books are for healing and that people learn about God and His Son Jesus. We also pray that someone, everyone get saved! My mother and I have such an awesome relationship with God and His Son Jesus and we want that for you too!

I know we are Christians and believe Jesus Christ is the way, but listen; we don't care what your faith is. We must all agree that God loves everyone and anyone can be encouraged.

We have added scriptures from the Old and New Testament of the Holy Bible. Therefore when you need to be encouraged you can just open our book. To God be the Glory!

OUR PRAYER

Always start with prayer!

JOHN 16:23-24

"AND IN THAT DAY YOU WILL ASK ME NOTHING. MOST ASSUREDLY, I SAY TO YOU, WHATEVER YOU ASK THE FATHER IN MY NAME HE WILL GIVE YOU. UNTIL NOW YOU HAVE ASKED NOTHING IN MY NAME. ASK, AND YOU WILL RECEIVE, THAT YOUR JOY MAY BE FULL.

OUR PRAYER

Heavenly Father,

We say thank you. Thank you for the gift of poetry to spread some love and to encourage others through ministry.

Our prayer is that people's lives will be touched and through our poetry it will also heal their hearts.

God we thank you most for the gift of poetry because writing our true feelings down saved both of our lives. Therefore, God we will honor You and always put You first.

Heavenly Father, we will serve You with our entire heart and we will praise You until we take our last breath.

You have covered my mother and I, no matter what life has dealt us and we are blessed. Once again, we say thank you.

In Jesus' name we pray. Amen.

John 16:23-24
"And in that day you will ask Me nothing. Most assuredly, I say to you, whatever you ask the Father in My name He will give you. Until now you have asked nothing in My name. Ask, and you will receive, that your joy may be full.

HELP ME GOD TO FILL MY FATHER'S SHOES

God, when I am feeling down and have the blues, encourage me to keep my head up. Help me God to fill my father's shoes.

1 KINGS 9:3

AND THE LORD SAID TO HIM, "I HAVE HEARD YOUR PRAYER AND YOUR SUPPLICATION, WHICH YOU HAVE MADE BEFORE ME; I HAVE CONSECRATED THIS HOUSE WHICH YOU HAVE BUILT, AND PUT MY NAME THERE FOREVER; MY EYES AND MY HEART WILL BE THERE FOR ALL-TIME.

HELP ME GOD TO FILL MY FATHER'S SHOES

Heavenly Father Above,

Protect and stay beside my father, this man that I love

He's leaving home to serve our country overseas;

I am his son a teenager, only fourteen

I am praying to You Heavenly Father

I am praying on my knees,

KEEP HIM SAFE FROM HARM PLEASE!

I am praying that I CAN FILL MY FATHER SHOES,

While he is serving his time in the military,

I have to be strong for my mother and siblings;

But I must admit this is scary

God, I know you would not give me more that I can bare

I am just thankful that You hear and answer prayers

God, keep Your Angels beside our family

Please Father; bring my daddy back home,

THESE ARE THE HEARTFELT WORDS THAT I PLEA!

(Continued)

HELP ME GOD TO FILL MY FATHER'S SHOES

Help me with each passing day

Help me set an example,

And have courage while my father is away

When my father writes or when he calls,

I pray that he is proud of me with NO WORRIES at all

God, when I am feeling down and have the blues;

Encourage me to keep my head up

HELP ME GOD TO FILL MY FATHER'S SHOES!

1 KINGS 9:3

AND THE LORD SAID TO HIM, "I HAVE HEARD YOUR PRAYER AND YOUR SUPPLICATION, WHICH YOU HAVE MADE BEFORE ME; I HAVE CONSECRATED THIS HOUSE WHICH YOU HAVE BUILT, AND PUT MY NAME THERE FOREVER; MY EYES AND MY HEART WILL BE THERE FOR ALL-TIME.

ON THE OUTSIDE LOOKING IN

Do not be too fast to give advice!

PSALMS 73:24

YOU WILL KEEP ON GUIDING ME WITH YOUR COUNSEL, LEADING ME TO A GLORIOUS DESTINY.

ON THE OUTSIDE LOOKING IN

When you are ON THE OUTSIDE LOOKING IN,

Caution...

Do not be too fast to give your advice

Be careful with your words,

Because you may just pay a price

When you are ON THE OUTSIDE LOOKING IN,

You should say less, pray more and just be a friend

You don't know where that person have been;

REMEMBER, YOU ARE ON THE OUTSIDE LOOKING IN

(God's Advice is Best!)

Psalms 73:24

You will keep on guiding me with your counsel, leading me to a glorious destiny.

YOU ARE THE ONE I CHOOSE

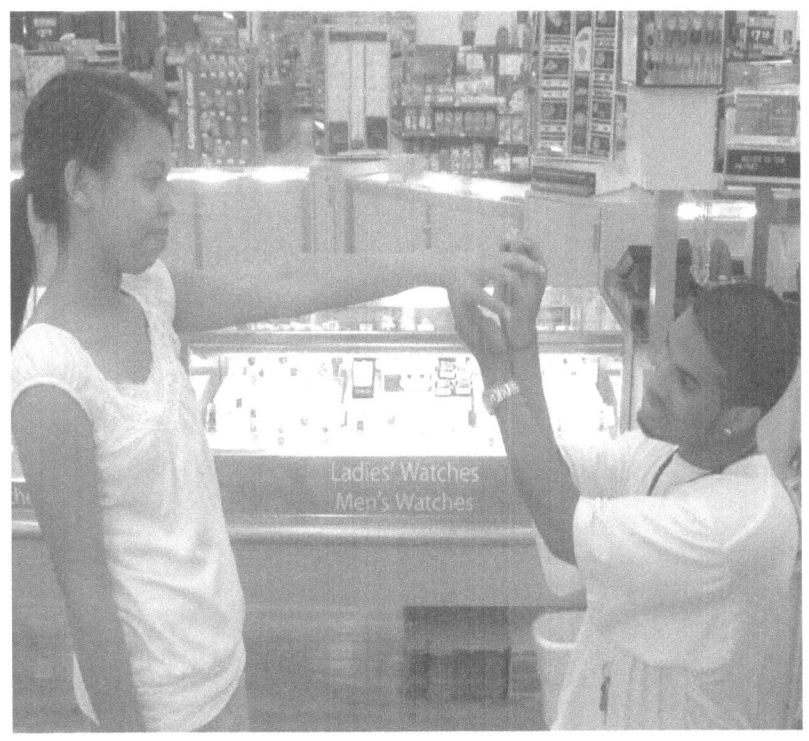

God made you for me; therefore I am grateful and blessed. You have filled my life with joy, love and happiness!

PROVERBS 18:22

HE WHO FINDS A WIFE FINDS A GOOD THING AND OBTAINS FAVOR FROM THE LORD.

YOU ARE THE ONE I CHOOSE

You are a special gift from God;

An Angel from above

You give me a gift daily and that gift is love

God made you for me;

Therefore, I am grateful and blessed

You have filled my life with joy, love and happiness!

Would you do me the honor in sharing my life?

Making me happy by becoming my wife

YOU ARE THE ONE I NEED

YOU ARE THE ONE I WANT

YOU ARE THE ONE I CHOOSE!

Proverbs 18:22

He who finds a wife finds a good thing and obtains favor from the Lord.

I WILL NOT PROCRASTINATE AGAIN

I sit and wonder why I started it late? Then I immediately fell to my knees and I asked for forgiveness because the Word of God tells us not to be lazy, which causes us to procrastinate.

HEBREWS 6:12
WE DO NOT WANT YOU TO BECOME LAZY, BUT TO IMITATE THOSE WHO THROUGH FAITH AND PATIENCE INHERIT WHAT HAS BEEN PROMISED.

I WILL NOT PROCRASTINATE AGAIN

I am urgently rushing,
Watching the clock to get my project done
I am making many mistakes,
I should have started my project days ago;
But, I chose to start it late!

I sit and wonder why I started it late?
Then I immediately fell to my knees and I asked for forgiveness,
Because the Word of God tells us not to be lazy
Which causes us to procrastinate

I may miss the deadline;
Why didn't I organize my time?
I promised myself, that when I did this in the past;
That time would be my last!

Although, I have said that almost everyday
I even got into the habit of asking God,
To help me how to organize, when I pray

(Continued)

I WILL NOT PROCRASTINATE AGAIN

I just think about the presser I feel,
And the unnecessary worry and concern
Waiting until the last minute;
Almost missing deadlines is a valuable lesson to learn!

Now I know it is up to me,
Not to procrastinate and set a goal
I must do it and be set free!

Therefore, I won't get stuck here;
I will learn from this, be obedient, overcome and win
I WILL NOT PROCRASTINATE, EVER AGAIN!

Hebrews 6:12
We do not want you to become lazy, but to imitate those who through faith and patience inherit what has been promised.

ECCLESIASTES 3:1-8 (NIV)

A Time for Everything

1 There is a time for everything, and a season for every activity under heaven:

2 a time to be born and a time to die,
   a time to plant and a time to uproot,

3 a time to kill and a time to heal,
   a time to tear down and a time to build,

4 a time to weep and a time to laugh, a time to mourn and a time to dance,

5 a time to scatter stones and a time to gather them,
   a time to embrace and a time to refrain,

6 a time to search and a time to give up,
   a time to keep and a time to throw away,

7 a time to tear and a time to mend,
   a time to be silent and a time to speak,

8 a time to love and a time to hate,
   a time for war and a time for peace.

KEEP YOUR HEAD UP

God did this for a reason
The storm has passed and now you must walk,
IN YOUR NEW SEASON!

KEEP YOUR HEAD UP AND KEEP YOUR FAITH IN GOD
His love is everlasting; He is by your side

So keep serving the Lord because this will heal your soul
Your life is a testimony that is worth more than gold

May this tribute help heal you and give you peace of mind
Your wounds and hurt will pass in time

SO BE ENCOURAGED TODAY AND ALWAYS,
You will live and see better days!

Therefore my friend, know you will rise again…
SO KEEP YOUR HEAD UP…SO YOU CAN WIN!

Psalm 3:3
But You, O LORD, are a shield for me, My glory and the One who lifts up my head.

SUFFERING THROUGH HURT OR PAIN

Suffering through pain,
Is like standing in a storm with no umbrella with pouring rain
While wondering when it's going to stop,
You feel sad and lonely, forgetting that sun will shine again
Suffering through hurt and you don't know what to do;
Sometimes you hurt so bad that it consumes you

Then you lay awake,
Thinking of what to do with your hurt or your pain;
Because they seem like they are one in the same
I'm sure that's how our Savior felt when we rejected Him,
And did not trust Him or call Him by name

When you are suffering with hurt or pain,
Jesus will make things better and grant you Eternal Life
The key to peace, love and happiness is simple...
JUST LOVE JESUS CHRIST!

Hebrew 2:11-18
Jesus can help through suffering.

CELEBRATE YOUR SPECIAL LOVE

You chose each other for the rest of your days, to love, to honor and to cherish now and for always.

EPHESIANS 5:22-23

WIVES, SUBMIT YOURSELVES TO YOUR HUSBANDS, AS TO THE LORD. FOR THE HUSBAND IS THE HEAD OF THE WIFE, AS CHRIST IS THE HEAD OF THE CHURCH, HIS BODY, OF WHICH HE IS THE SAVIOR.

CELEBRATE YOUR SPECIAL LOVE

May your marriage be blessed and filled with happiness
May today bring unity to both your families
You chose each other for the rest of your days,
TO LOVE, TO HONOR AND TO CHERISH ALWAYS

May your wedding day be extra special,
And bring you blessed joy
If I searched the whole world through,
I could not find two people who would deserve it more!

God is smiling down and Heavens Angels are rejoicing above,
To celebrate your special love

I know your family and guests are honored to be there,
To share these special memories with you
May God bless you on your wedding day
AND BLESS YOUR MARRIAGE TOO!

Ephesians 5:22-23

Wives, submit yourselves to your husbands, as to the Lord. For the husband is the head of the wife, as Christ is the head of the church, His body, of which He is the Savior.

WE ALL NEED TO GIVE LOVE

Love instead of hate, is the only way
WE ALL NEED TO GIVE LOVE AND ALWAYS PRAY!

PRAY FOR PEACE,
Pray for so many people who are suffering today

Open your heart too,
THIS IS WHAT JESUS WOULD DO!

Romans 12:10

Be kindly affectionate to one another with brotherly love, in honor giving preference to one another.

GOD CAN FORGIVE THE ADULTERER

GOD CAN FORGIVE THE ADULTERER,
But you must be sincere in your heart

You cannot be lukewarm on the subject of adultery,
Or confused on what to do
The relationship must be over and the feelings gone too!

I am not preaching to you on what to do
I'M JUST IT MAKING PLAIN…
On what the Holy Spirit tells me what to share with you

Simply, adultery is foolish and hurtful;
AND HAS CONSEQUENCES!

God considers lust just as sinful as adultery
Although God forbids adultery, God can forgive the adulterer

BE BLESSED AND STOP THE FOOLISHNESS!

Matthew 5:28
But I say unto you that whosoever looks at a woman to lust for her has already committed adultery with her in his heart.

YOU WILL SEE YOUR HUSBAND AGAIN

I was deeply hurt and sadden to hear,
Your husband has passed away
I want to encourage you that in time, your heart will heal
And the pain you feel gets easier, you will see a better day!

Sometimes we need strength to continue to hold on,
Just know your husband is in a better place
Not even death, can take away the love you both shared;
Your love can never be replaced!

But, one thing is for certain…
The love for your husband will remain the same
A piece of him will always stay with you,
Most importantly, the memories will always remain

God took your husband to his Heavenly home,
But He promises to take care of you…
You'll never be alone!

Just know death is not the end,
YOU WILL SEE YOUR HUSBAND AGAIN

1 Thessalonians 4:13-14

Death is not the end of a person.

I SHOULD BE DEAD

You beat me for the very last time. Don't you realize you are committing a crime?

PSALMS 12:5
GOD PROTECTS THOSE WHO ARE HELPLESS.

I SHOULD BE DEAD

Eleven years of marriage thrown away,

Just because you could not stop hitting me everyday!

You beat me for the last time

Don't you realize you are committing a crime?

You say you love me and you won't do it again

But nothing changes,

Therefore I must be my own best friend

I must go away,

Where you cannot hurt me anymore

I know you think these are just words,

Because you heard them before

Well, this time it's true

I am not taking another beating,

I'M LEAVING YOU!

(Continued)

I SHOULD BE DEAD

Please don't try to find me,
You'll be wasting your time
Just let me go,
So I can have peace of mind

I do not hate you,
I wish you the best
The fact that I can walk out of here,
I am blessed!

According to my injuries, past doctor visits
And the knots on my head;
I SHOULD NOT BE HERE…I SHOULD BE DEAD!

Psalms 12:5
God protects those who are helpless.

MY SECRET

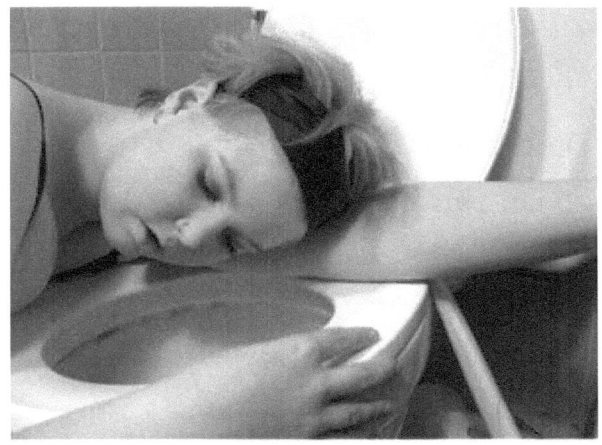

No one knows my secret I keep. I have an illness called Bulimia, I purge after I eat.

PSALM 44:21

WOULD NOT GOD HAVE DISCOVERED IT, SINCE HE KNOWS THE SECRETS OF THE HEART?

MY SECRET

When I look in the mirror, what do I see?
A disgusting image looking back at me!
I look so fat; I am extremely depressed and unhappy

Every time I see myself, I start to cry
I don't understand and I try to figure out why?
Why do I hate myself and have low self-esteem?
When no one else sees me this way;
And, no one has teased me to be mean

No one knows MY SECRET I KEEP,
I have an illness called BULIMIA, I PURGE AFTER I EAT
When I am in public…I pretend everything is fine,
I even appear happy most of the time

I started out just trying to lose a few pounds and had no success
THE WEIGHT WAS NOT COMING OFF FAST ENOUGH,
That is how I got started in this mess!

Purging is unhealthy, but I can't stop it

(Continued)

MY SECRET

The reason is because, I love the new me!
This is the image I want the world to see

I am a size 4 and people tell me I look great
But the way I got this way...I really hate!
I know I need to go to the doctors or seek therapy,
Therefore my mind can be clear and set free!

Free from my secret and lying to myself,
I need to get well and eat right for my health
I need to start now because I am near death
If I believe otherwise I am fooling myself!

I'm making a wise decision,
Because this Bulimia is getting out of hand
I will no longer purge and from this day forward,
FOR GOOD HEALTH I STAND!

Bulimia is an eating disorder. Someone with Bulimia might binge on food and then vomit (also called purge) in a cycle of binging and purging.

Psalm 44:21

Would not God have discovered it, since He knows the secrets of the heart?

PASSAGE PSALM 63:1-8

Psalm 63 A psalm of David. When he was in the Desert of Judah.

1. O God, you are my God, earnestly I seek you; my soul thirsts for you, my body longs for you, in a dry and weary land where there is no water.

2. I have seen you in the sanctuary and beheld your power and your glory.

3. Because your love is better than life, my lips will glorify you.

4. I will praise you as long as I live, and in your name I will lift up my hands.

5. My soul will be satisfied as the richest of foods; with singing lips my mouth will praise you.

6. On my bed I remember you; I think of you through the watches of the night.

7. Because you are my help, I sing in the shadow of your wings.

8. My soul follows close behind You; Your right hand upholds me

COVER ME LORD!

Cover me Lord, both night and day
These are the words in Jesus' name I humbly pray

Cover me and my family Lord at all times
Even when we fall short and go astray,
Also, cover the officers on the street from harms way

Cover the soldiers Lord that is protecting our country
So we can feel safe to take a simple walk,
Or play with our children in the park

Cover everyone Lord that reads this book and their needs,
You supply them all
Added with peace, mercy and grace
Pick them up when they fall

Please continue to Cover me Lord,
As I do my part to minister to lost or hurting souls
If I can reach only one, that will be worth more than gold!

(Continued)

COVER ME LORD

I will serve You, I will fast and I will pray

I will always carry my Bible,

Because my Bible is my Sword

I will put my trust in You for everything so…

PLEASE COVER ME LORD!

Deuteronomy 33:12

The beloved of the Lord shall dwell in safety by him; and the Lord shall cover him all the day long and he shall dwell between his shoulders.

KEEP CHRIST IN CHRISTMAS

Keep Christ in Christmas wouldn't you agree? Explain to your children, Christmas means more than gifts and a tree.

PSALM 100:4
ENTER INTO HIS GATES WITH THANKSGIVING, AND INTO HIS COURTS WITH PRAISE: BE THANKFUL UNTO HIM, AND BLESS HIS NAME.

KEEP CHRIST IN CHRISTMAS

Keep Christ in Christmas wouldn't you agree?
Explain to your children,
CHRISTMAS MEANS MORE THAN GIFTS AND A TREE

Remember to pray and give thanks for our Savior above
Survive the season by sharing, caring and spreading lots of love

Love for your neighbor and family,
Should be on the top of your list
Pick up the telephone or send a card to people you miss
This is a time for giving even if it is only a hug and a kiss

WHATEVER YOU DO KEEP CHRIST IN CHRISTMAS;
And you cannot go wrong
Just be thankful because you are blessed,
REMEMBER THAT ALL-DAY LONG!

Psalm 100:4

Enter into His gates with thanksgiving, and into His courts with praise: be thankful unto Him, and bless His name.

PICK YOUR WEEDS

If you want your Garden to Grow,
PICK YOUR WEEDS

If you want your Ministry to Grow,
SOW A SEED

If you want to be Abundantly Blessed,
HELP SOMEONE IN NEED

But to have the Gift of Discernment,
PRAY TO GOD TO INTERCEDE

When you need to be Delivered from People,
SIMPLY PICK YOUR WEEDS!

Psalm 119:125

I am your servant; give me discernment that I may understand your statutes.

SERENITY PRAYER

God grant me the serenity to accept the things
I cannot change;
Courage to change the things I can;
And wisdom to know the difference.

Living one day at a time;
Enjoying one moment at a time;

Accepting hardships as the pathway to peace;
Taking as He did, this sinful world as it is,
Not as I would have it;

Trusting that He will make all things right if
I surrender to His will;
That I may be reasonably happy in this life and
Supremely happy with Him. Amen.

Reinhold Niebuhr/1943.

No-one is totally sure who wrote this prayer, although Reinhold Niebuhr is often credited with it. However, some link it with Friedrich Oetinger, an 18th century theologian, while others attribute the prayer to the Roman philosopher Boethius, living in the early part of the sixth century.

A VICTIM OF 9/11

(This a fictional story)

I woke up this morning;
And the sun was shinning brighter than I ever seen
I got up out of bed and took a shower, did my normal routine
While I was getting dress for work, I started to pray
Pray that God would bless me and my family this day

I go into the kitchen to get a bite to eat
I read the newspaper,
And then I slipped my shoes onto my feet
It is time to go to work...So I kissed my wife and kids
I grabbed my briefcase and now I am on my way
I waive good-bye, as I walked to my car to start my day

I drove for about forty minutes, singing to the radio
I pulled up to my building and parked my car,
Walked to the elevator and pushed the button to the 23rd floor

(Continued)

A VICTIM OF 9/11

(This a fictional story)

While working later that day…I heard someone say,
"Planes from the sky are headed our way!"

The next thing I knew,
Myself and others fell down on the floor
Then I was left breathless…Do I say more?

To the Families

Although this story is not real, this is only a sample of a day of a victim of 9/11 may feel. We have no idea what any of the victims went through. Nevertheless, the pain and suffering of the loss is very real. I just wanted to take the time to let the families of the victims know that we care about them and what 9/11 has done to me and you. Please know that God has your loved ones in His Hands, may He send protective Angels to cover you. September 11th will never be forgotten. This is in memory of all of the families.

2 Corinthians 1:3

Blessed be God, even the Father of our Lord Jesus Christ, the Father of mercies, and the God of all comfort.

PICK UP YOUR BED AND WALK

Do not feel down, sad, depressed or paralyzed. Just pick up your bed and walk.

JOHN 5:8
JESUS SAID TO HIM, "RISE, TAKE UP YOUR BED AND WALK."

PICK UP YOUR BED AND WALK

When you feel down from suffering and pain
When you feel like your life has no meaning
Therefore, you feel depressed again

It has been along time that anything has changed,
It has been years
When you think about this,
Your eyes immediately are filled up with tears

Do not cry and do not worry for God sees all
When you need answers;
Anytime, day or night; on Him you can call

The answers He will give you is,
Do not feel down, sad, depressed or paralyzed
Just pick up your bed and walk

Walk into your future, which is a better day
That is what you will get when you go to your Father,
In Jesus' name and pray!

(Continued)

PICK UP YOUR BED AND WALK

Depression is not an option,
When you are a Child of God

Therefore, turn it over to Him quickly;
YOU WILL FEEL BETTER INSIDE!

John 5:8
Jesus said to him, "Rise, take up thy bed and walk."

Isaiah 60:1
Arise from the depression and prostration in which circumstances have kept you--rise to a new life! Shine (be radiant with the glory of the Lord), for your light has come, and the glory of the Lord has risen upon you!

ANOTHER WOMEN YOU CALL WIFE

I saw this card and I thought of you,
It was painful but yet it was true

I could not believe you did not call me after our first date
I just knew everything went great

I found out later…
You are married and have kids
Why did you keep this information from me?
Having a wife you purposely hid

I know we get disappointed from people in this life
Now I know it was wrong for us to date,
Because you belong to…
ANOTHER WOMAN YOU CALL WIFE!

Exodus 20:14
You shall not commit adultery.

ATTEMP OF SUICIDE

I was seriously depressed and the feelings would not go away. I cried so hard but did not pray. I just wanted it to end; therefore I took the pills; to end my life this day.

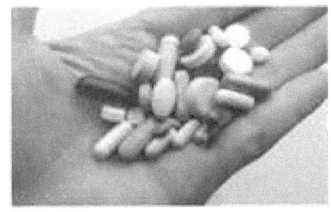

REVELATION 21:4

AND GOD SHALL WIPE AWAY ALL TEARS FROM THEIR EYES; AND THERE SHALL BE NO MORE DEATH, NEITHER SORROW, NOR CRYING, NEITHER SHALL THERE BE ANY MORE PAIN: FOR THE FORMER THINGS ARE PASSED AWAY.

ATTEMP OF SUICIDE

(A fictional story based on facts)

I was seriously depressed and the feelings would not go away

I cried so hard but did not pray

I just wanted it to end; therefore I took the pills;

To end my life this day

My wife and children needing me did come to my mind

Now the room is getting darker;

Does this mean, I'm running out of time?

Time to decide if I want to live;

Or did I want to go?

Could I reverse the damage I've done?

My real emotions of fear are starting to grow!

I am severely weak,

Trying to crawl to the telephone

I am starting to lose consciousness and I'm all alone

By the Grace of God,

I was able to get to the telephone and call for help

(Continued)

ATTEMPT OF SUICIDE

(A fictional story based on facts)

As my voice weakens and starts to fade…
I heard the women say, "She is sending someone to my aid!"

The next thing I remember,
Is waking up with tubes down my throat
I was feeling blessed that my life was saved,
However, I was still depressed and at the end of my rope!

The doctor walks in the hospital room to inform me,
That I am mentally ill
And the only way I will survive this…
Is possibly with medication but it must be God's Will!

Since there was nothing left for me to do,
But to lay there and pray
I used my strength to thank God,
That I survived to see another day

I understand that life is a precious gift and I waited to late,
To discuss my issues and be honest about my depression;
To remove this heavy weight

(Continued)

ATTEMPT OF SUICIDE

(A fictional story based on facts)

I was more concerned about,
What everyone would think about me
Instead of being honest and setting myself free!

I realize depression is a Demon that I have to fight
No one understands how difficult it is,
Just to get through just one night

Therefore, I'm turning this depression over to God!
Finally, I can have peace inside
NEVER, NEVER AGAIN….WILL I ATTEMPT SUICIDE!

Parents, Children with Suffering with Mental Illness or need a Pediatrician that cares Contact: The Bethesda Clinic Inc. (Glorifying God through Spirit, Soul & Body) 1148 Pulaski Highway Suite 107-317 Bear, Delaware 19701. They can be reached at 302-266-0591 or by E-mail: info@thebethesdaclinic.com

Revelation 21:4

And God shall wipe away all tears from their eyes; and there shall be no more death, neither sorrow, nor crying, neither shall there be any more pain: for the former things are passed away.

A MOTHER WITH AN URGENT PRAYER

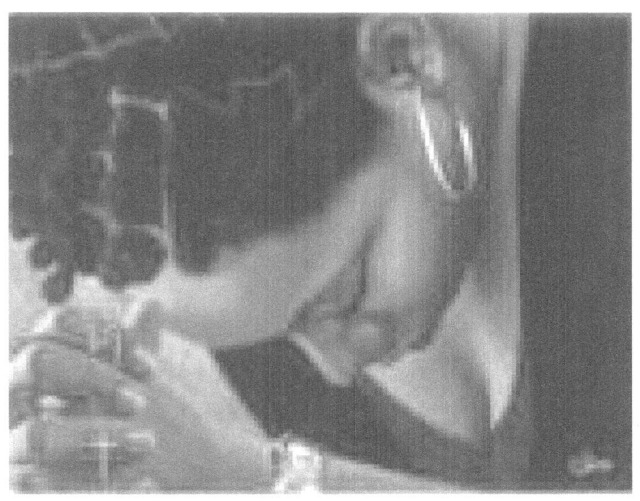

Father, I'm a mother with an urgent prayer. I stretch my hand to Thee, no other help I know. Down on my knees, is the only place left to go.

ISAIAH 30:19

HE WILL BE VERY GRACIOUS UNTO THEE AT THE VOICE OF THY CRY; WHEN HE SHALL HEAR IT, HE WILL ANSWER THEE.

A MOTHER WITH AN URGENT PRAYER

Father, I'm a mother with an urgent prayer

I stretch my hand to Thee, no other help I know

Down on my knees, is the only place left to go!

I did seek You first;

But back then, my life was full of sin

That's why You did not hear me Father,

Now I have been redeemed and I am calling on You again!

My daughter is on the street,

Selling her body to every man she meets…

For alcohol, drugs and/or money to eat

I have reached out to her, letting her know;

I would take care of her

Also, any of her needs I would happily provide,

Because what she is doing to her life and her body

Is killing me slowly inside

God, I know You have the Master Plan

And everything is in Your hands

(Continued)

A MOTHER WITH AN URGENT PRAYER

God, I do trust You but I am scared;
Because she has been gone for so long
Please help me Father,
Bring my daughter safely home!

God, I do not know what else to do;
But to let go of my child and give her back to You

I'll let go and let God;
Therefore, please heal the pain I feel inside

Father, things cannot be clearer;
I AM A MOTHER WITH AN URGENT PRAYER!

Isaiah 30:19
He will be very gracious unto Thee at the voice of thy cry; when He shall hear it, He will answer thee.

PEACE AND LOVE WITHIN

If you are searching for PEACE,
And you don't know what to do
First ask your Father in Heaven,
To give you peace and love inside of you

The scripture Isaiah 26:3 says,
You will keep him in perfect peace whose mind is stayed on You
This is a scripture to memorize,
Because you will remember that God cares about you

When you have PEACE, you will not cry anymore
Instead, you will be calm and happy;
The true emotions you are searching for

Pray for peace in your heart, it makes you easier to love
Because when love comes from the heart, peace rushes in
YOU WILL FEEL PEACE AND LOVE WITHIN

Philippians 4:7
And the peace of God, which surpasses all understanding, will guard your hearts and minds through Christ Jesus.

YOUR TEARS ARE ONLY TEMPORARY

This too shall pass, your hardship won't last. No need to get weary, your tears are only temporary.

PSALM 126:5
THEY THAT SOW IN TEARS SHALL REAP IN JOY.

YOUR TEARS ARE ONLY TEMPORARY

This too shall pass, your hardship won't last
No need to get weary, your tears are only temporary

Tell yourself, I will cry no longer
Crying is not always a sign of weakness,
It can make you stronger

Crying can bring on stress and it can be a big price to pay
Therefore, find some happiness and do it soon
Not tomorrow, find happiness today!

Start by wiping your tears away,
Then ask God what you should do differently;
Or change when you pray?

Apply the change to your life each and everyday
God does not want His children to suffer in anyway!

Always, remember that this too shall pass;
Your hardship won't last
No need to get weary,
YOUR TEARS ARE ONLY TEMPORARY!

Psalm 126:5
They that sow in tears shall reap in joy.

MY LIFE IS IN YOUR HANDS

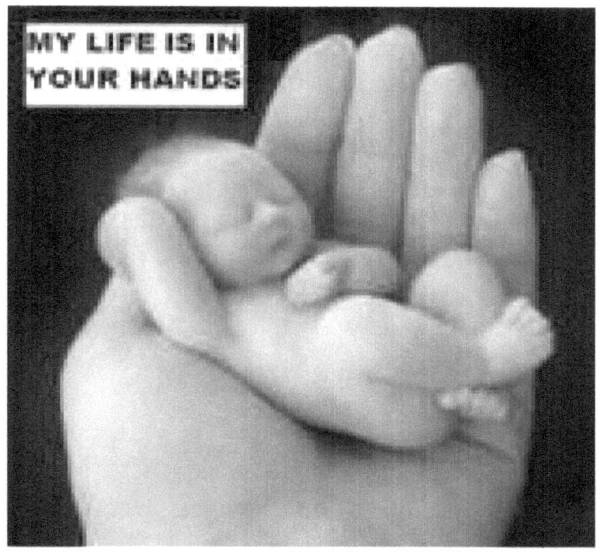

Don't you know mommy that life started, as soon as you made me! I know this is something you will not fully understand. That does not even matter. What does matter mommy, is my life is in your hands!

GOD CARES FOR THE UNBORN

PSALM 139:13

FOR YOU CREATED MY INMOST BEING; YOU KNIT ME TOGETHER IN MY MOTHER'S WOMB.

MY LIFE IS IN YOUR HANDS

Life has just begun
You don't even know it yet but you are my mommy,
And I am your son

I must stay in the womb, so I can grow
How you will react to the news,
I really don't know?

Mom, last night I was conceived
Now, my life is in your hands if I stay or leave

I know I am unexpected, but God do not make mistakes
I also know I was not planned, but mommy I could not wait!

I could not wait to be your child
So please let me grow inside of you mommy,
The way God intended and leave me alone
Therefore I can be born to you and apart of your home

(Continued)

MY LIFE IS IN YOUR HANDS

Nine months from now, I'll be introduced to you
Just as long as you don't abort me mommy,
Like you planned too!

It would be so sad that I knew you,
But my face you will never get to see

Don't you know mommy that life started,
As soon as you made me?

I know this is something you will not fully understand
That does not even matter,
What does matter mommy is,
MY LIFE IS IN YOUR HANDS!

GOD CARES FOR THE UNBORN

Psalm 139:13

For You created my inmost being, You knit me together in my mother's womb.

I BELIEVE GOD

I BELIEVE GOD, through life storms, the suffering and pain
I BELIEVE GOD, for my soul…In Jesus' name

I BELIEVE GOD, for all of my blessings,
For joy and peace of mind
I just believe God for everything,
Because I trust Him that everything will turn out fine

I BELIEVE GOD, for complete healing,
And I praise Him for everything He has already done
I BELIEVE GOD, that the victory has already been won!

I BELIEVE GOD, for I know He is in control of my life
I know there is no battle of mine He will not fight

I BELIEVE GOD, with my entire heart and soul,
His love endures forever and is worth more than gold!

I BELIEVE GOD and His Word, I'll try to live the right way
I just want to get into Heaven on Judgment Day
I BELIEVE GOD!

2 Corinthians 5:7
For we walk by faith and not by sight.

IN HEAVEN ALL-DAY

I went home to be with the Lord,
Now I'm here in Heaven all-day

I see you often grieving for me,
But to be absent from the body is to be present with the Lord

You see, I am happy, truly happy
Because I sit with the Father and Jesus
Surrounded by Angels *(Hallelujah Praise His Name)*

Worshipping God all-day long,
Singing all my favorite songs

I'll see you when you get here, until then…
I'll be rejoicing with my new Best Friend

I want for nothing, no worries, no pain
Everything my Father promised was here when I came

(Continued)

IN HEAVEN ALL-DAY

Peace, serenity, love and worship all-day long
I lift my hands to give thanks,
That my good deeds out weighed my wrong

I am so grateful that I was saved,
And I did not wait to long

Also, that I accepted the Lord as my Savior,
Now I call Heaven my home!

Jesus is the name I shout and in His name I pray
I just praise the Lord and have a good time,
IN HEAVEN ALL-DAY!

1 Thessalonians 4:16

For the Lord Himself will come down from Heaven, with a loud command, with the voice of the archangel and with the trumpet call of God, and the dead in Christ will rise first.

I WAIT FOR THE KEY TO TURN

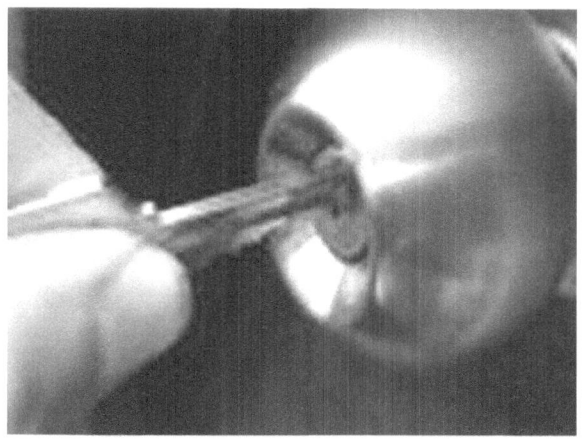

This relationship has been a hard lesson to learn. I have decided that this is the last night I will wait for the key to turn!

MATTHEW 11:25
AND WHEN YOU STAND PRAYING, IF YOU HOLD ANYTHING AGAINST ANYONE, FORGIVE HIM, SO THAT YOUR FATHER IN HEAVEN MAY FORGIVE YOUR SINS.

I WAIT FOR THE KEY TO TURN

The sun is starting to come up, as I wait for the key to turn
Why do I continue to believe him?
When will I ever learn?

Maybe I want to believe he will change,
Because I have loved him all of my life
Maybe because in my heart I believe things will get better
Or because I need him or because I am his wife

While waiting for the key to turn, I'm pacing the floor
I see a car approaching and I run to the door
No, that car is moving to fast, that is not him!
I can't stand it, I can't take it anymore!

I fall to my knees and yell Father please!
What woman has my husband out all hours of the night?
God, this is not a battle I want to continue to fight!

Although right now I'm angry and hurt
There is nothing else for me to do but wait and pray
Pray that he will come home to me,
And not in the street where he often stay

(Continued)

I WAIT FOR THE KEY TO TURN

God, I hear Your Voice loud and clear
She is nothing special,
Just easy pleasure, he will be back by mid-day

God, I hear you telling me,
That my husband is not leaving me for another woman
This is just a game he likes to play

In fact, he enjoys having me waiting for the key to turn
He knows that I am here doing nothing but sitting,
And waiting for him to come home

Therefore, God since I know all of this is true,
I will let go and turn this over to You

I hope my husband understands what he is doing is not right
Most importantly, I am becoming ill,
And I can't take this pain anymore tonight!

I am going to say a prayer and go to sleep
I know in my heart that whatever anyone sows, they will reap!

(Continued)

I WAIT FOR THE KEY TO TURN

I don't wish harm on my husband because he is still my mate
I am praying that I can forgive him,
And truly love him before it is too late

I know the Lord brought us together,
And I don't want it to end
I thought I married my true best friend

Every month we go through something,
And I have to forgive him
Forgive him for adultery or emotional abuse
Sometimes I just throw my hands up and say,
"What's the use?"

This relationship has been filled with hard lessons to learn
I have decided that this is the last night,
I WILL WAIT FOR THE KEY TO TURN!

Matthew 11:25

And when you stand praying, if you hold anything against anyone, forgive him, so that your Father in heaven may forgive your sins.

GOD RELEASED MY SPIRITUALS GIFTS

God released my Spiritual Gifts
Since then my life to others seem unorganized
But I just had so much on my plate

I tried to take off just one or two things,
Therefore I can concentrate

I tried to figure out what I can do,
To relieve some pressure and weight

God want us to be focused,
Not having us all over the place
Not giving our best or 100% is a waste!

God does not Get the Glory,
Most importantly, your results will tell the story!

Therefore, when you ask God to release your gifts,
BE READY FOR YOUR LIFE TO SHIFT

(Continued)

GOD RELEASED MY SPIRITUALS GIFTS

I have learned how to multi-task,
But when I need help, I am not afraid to ask

I am a Women of God that serves the church,
I am also mother, wife and publisher to name a few
Therefore being overwhelmed is easy to do

When God released my Spiritual Gifts, I asked who?
HE REPLIED, YOU!

1 Corinthians 14:12

Even so you, since you are zealous for spiritual gifts, let it be for the edification of the church that you seek to excel.

FIND MY DADDY WHO LOOKS LIKE ME

I am just a little kid standing at the window and looking everyday. I am trying to find my daddy, he just up and left us one day. What I am going to do, is pray to God and ask Him to please...Please find my daddy, who looks like me!

To all single parents I am proud of you! If you are not in your child's life, please search your heart and change.

ISAIAH 58:9

THEN YOU SHALL CALL, AND THE LORD WILL ANSWER; YOU SHALL CRY, AND HE WILL SAY, 'HERE I AM.'

FIND MY DADDY WHO LOOKS LIKE ME

I am just a little kid,

Standing at the window and looking everyday

I am trying to find my daddy,

He just up and left us one day

My mommy is trying to be both mommy and daddy,

And raise me right

She is trying not to show it,

But I hear her crying herself to sleep at night

I don't understand why he left us?

I wonder if he ever thinks about me?

What I am going to do, is pray to God

And ask Him to please...

PLEASE FIND MY DADDY, WHO LOOKS LIKE ME!

Isaiah 58:9

Then you shall call, and the LORD will answer; You shall cry, and He shall say, 'Here I am.'

GOD'S WILL

We always use the statement, "If it's God's Will."
DO WE REALLY MEAN IT?

Do we really turn everything over to Him,
AND LET GO AND LET GOD?

When we need to hear from Him,
DO WE STAY COMPLETELY STILL?

Do you know the difference between your thoughts,
AND HIS VOICE?

Children of God, if you do...
You will always make the correct choice

However, if you are filled with doubt or lack of faith,
Then your life can be filled with uneasiness and confusion,
AND ONLY GOD KNOWS YOUR FATE

(Continued)

GOD'S WILL

Therefore, be honest with yourself
And daily review your flesh

Start living in God's Will
Because He truly knows what's best

Put your complete trust in Him
Be thankful for life, be obedient,
AND LET GOD ORDER YOUR STEPS

Your life will be in complete harmony and fulfilled
YOU WILL BE WALKING IN GOD'S WILL!

1 Thessalonians 5:18
Be thankful in all circumstances, for this is God's will for you who belong to Christ Jesus.

GOD DOESN'T MAKE MISTAKES

BARACK OBAMA ELECTED AS THE 44TH PRESIDENT OF THE UNITED STATES ON NOVEMBER 4TH 2008

YES WE CAN! YES WE DID!

PHILIPPIANS 3:14
I PRESS TOWARD THE MARK FOR THE PRIZE OF THE HIGH CALLING OF GOD IN CHRIST JESUS.

GOD DOESN'T MAKE MISTAKES

Everyone was patient while they stood in long lines,
Some of them waited for hours to vote
Most of them had pride and did not mind
They knew something had to change,
And voting for Barack Obama gave them new hope!

Change is what we desperately need in our land
That's why we voted for the candidate that had the better plan

America voted on November 4th to elect the 44th President
Our voices were heard and history was made
What we witnessed was a miracle,
And now we have heartfelt memories that will never fade

Barack Obama was elected to serve our country,
For at least four years
Every time I think about this blessing,
Brings my eyes to tears

(Continued)

GOD DOESN'T MAKE MISTAKES

Everyone knows that Barack Obama cares
For our country, which is easy to see
Barack is also a righteous man,
That has good morals and integrity

Dr. Martin Luther King had a dream, now the dream lives
Barack Obama will keep the dream alive, with the service he gives

He has four years to try to fix years of oppression
Along with ending the war in Iraq;
And stopping a great depression

That is why we need to be unified,
Show love; give respect, honor and appreciation
Because Barack Obama's job will not be easy,
Starting with the hurting economy that is in need of restoration

We have a chance to support our President;
And help him to get things right
We must remember that no change will come overnight

We must help him fight for freedom and justice for all,
God has ordained him to answer this call

(Continued)

GOD DOESN'T MAKE MISTAKES

So let's stand together and keep the spirit alive!
The same energy and power used to vote him into office,
Is what we need in the coming years to survive

We are about to take an amazing journey
I am grateful that Barack Obama will lead the way
Everyone must do their part and continue to constantly pray
Pray that America will be different,
That change will come and we see a better day

Some people say he won because he was lucky,
Instead of admitting that it was fate

Our God doesn't need luck,
He Just commands that His will be done
GOD DOESN'T MAKE MISTAKES!

Our tribute to Barack Obama

Philippians 3:14
I press toward the mark for the prize of the high calling of God in Christ Jesus.

HE WILL NEVER ABANDON YOU

Hold on to your Fathers love and when you feel lonely reach out for Him or call for Him whenever you can. You will feel secure in knowing, you can reach out for His hand.

DEUTERONOMY 31:8

THE LORD HIMSELF GOES BEFORE YOU AND WILL BE WITH YOU; HE WILL NEVER LEAVE YOU NOR FORSAKE YOU. DO NOT BE AFRAID; DO NOT BE DISCOURAGED."

HE WILL NEVER ABANDON YOU

You are never alone, God is always near
There is no need to feel abandoned or live in fear

God walks with you every step of the way,
Let Him order your steps everyday

Never feel unwanted because that is never true
God completely loves His children and is concerned,
HE WILL NEVER ABANDON YOU

You are special and unique,
Your relationship with God should be one of a kind
It should always give you comfort,
Most importantly, give you peace of mind

Hold on to Your Fathers love
When you feel lonely, reach out for Him;
Or call for Him whenever you can

You will feel secure in knowing,
YOU CAN REACH OUT FOR HIS HAND

(Continued)

HE WILL NEVER ABANDON YOU

You are never alone;
God is only a prayer away

He loves you UNCONDITIONALLY
Love that will never go and will always stay!

Please know even when God is disappointed in you,
There is no sin too great, no matter what you do

Just repent and always have faith in the God you serve,
BECAUSE HE WOULD NEVER ABANDON YOU!

Deuteronomy 31:8

The LORD Himself goes before you and will be with you; He will never leave you nor forsake you. Do not be afraid; do not be discouraged."

WILL YOU CHANGE?

Will you change or remain the same?
CHANGE FROM THE INSIDE OUT?

Your outside appearance may look great
But don't try to fool others by acting fake
Pretending you are something that you are not,
Don't make that big mistake!

Remember there is nothing you can hide
Everything you do is recorded, we can't fool God!

Therefore, will you change or continue to remain the same?
Understand, you reap what you sow,
You only will have yourself to blame

GOD, WANTS A PURE HEART
Therefore please repent, that is where you start
Then take it day by day, learning a new way
Not doing things the same!
I ask you again, WILL YOU CHANGE?

Acts 3:19

Repent ye therefore, and be converted, that your sins may be blotted out, when the times of refreshing shall come from the presence of the Lord.

WHAT ABOUT ME?

I wake up daily depressed, wanting to kill myself to be set free!
Because no one understands why I ask the question,
WHAT ABOUT ME?

I was born female but inside I feel like a male,
This secret lives inside of me with no one to talk to,
No one to tell

People use to call me a tomboy,
Now they call me Weird, Crazy and Gay!
I no longer want to be different or to live this way

I want to be normal; this is the prayer I give to God
Because I want to feel happy,
If just for a moment, feel like boy inside

I want no mean comments on MySpace
I don't want any judgmental people in my face!

I want to hear from others,
That I am going to Heaven and not Hell

(Continued)

WHAT ABOUT ME?

I want to hear a doctor say...I am no longer sick,
I'm healthy and well

That's why I am always crying,
And I want to die to be set free
Now can't you see why I ask the question,
WHAT ABOUT ME?

I did not choose this, I was born this way
I am Transgender, I am not Gay!

Therefore please do not judge or be mean,
But pray that I am no longer confused or want to hurt myself

Pray that my mind is set FREE
While I continue to ask the question...
WHAT ABOUT ME?

2 Chronicles 30:9
For the Lord your God is gracious and merciful, and will not turn away His face from you, if ye return to Him.

THE LORD'S PRAYER

Psalm 23 (New King James Version)

A Psalm of David.

1 The LORD *is* my shepherd;
I shall not want.

2 He makes me to lie down in green pastures;
He leads me beside the still waters.

3 He restores my soul;
He leads me in the paths of righteousness
For His name's sake.

4 Yea, though I walk through the valley of the shadow of death,
I will fear no evil; For You *are* with me;
Your rod and Your staff, they comfort me.

5 You prepare a table before me in the presence of my enemies;
You anoint my head with oil; My cup runs over.

6 Surely goodness and mercy shall follow me All the days of my life; And I will dwell in the house of the LORD Forever.

I HAVE A TESTIMONY

I have a testimony because God has set me free; I thank God because now I can live and be what He has called me to be.

JOB 5:9
HE DOES GREAT THINGS TOO MARVELOUS TO UNDERSTAND. HE PERFORMS COUNTLESS MIRACLES.

I HAVE A TESTIMONY

If I did not have such a troubled past,
If I did not have some misery
If I did not need to be delivered,
I would not have a testimony!

I have a testimony because God has set me free
I thank God because now I can live,
And be what He has called me to be

I can walk in my purpose and let my light shine
I can do this because God is with me,
And He gives me peace of mind

I no longer live in darkness, in depression…
Or with feelings of heavy weight

Instead, I live with joy and excitement;
To see what God has planned for my fate

No more suicidal thought of death,
Due to extreme amounts of stress

(Continued)

I HAVE A TESTIMONY

I live a victorious life,
I life with purpose, a life that's blessed!

I want you to know that my life is focused on one purpose,
Pressed toward one goal

To be Christ-like and be the best servant
And minister to the world to heal their hearts,
And deliver lost souls

I will tell everyone about Jesus Christ, my Savior;
How He has delivered me

Most importantly,
I will tell them how He gave me a purpose
He showed me how to write and publish poetry

He healed my body,
NOW I HAVE A TESTIMONY!

Job 5:9

He does great things too marvelous to understand. He performs countless miracles.

PREPARING FOR BAPTISM

"TAKE ME TO THE WATER TO BE BAPTIZED"

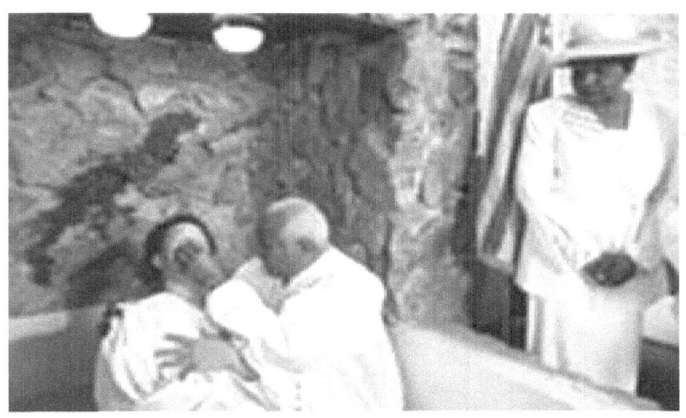

Baptism means throwing away the old person and becoming a new person spiritually. Also, you have accepted Jesus as your personal Savior.

MATTHEW 3:11
BAPTISM SIGNIFIES REPENTANCE.

PREPARING FOR BAPTISM

"Take Me to the Water to be Baptized." We all know that favorite hymn. Baptism is one of the most beautiful ceremonies I have ever seen. I love to help the candidates prepare for baptism.

A lot of people are afraid of being baptized or think it is just a ceremony, so it's not necessary. If Jesus thought it was necessary, then you must re-think your decision and GET BAPTIZED!

Baptism means throwing away the old person and becoming a new person spiritually. Also, that you have accepted Jesus as your personal Savior. It is a blessing for you to get baptized in the public for your family, friends and whomever comes to see.

Now, you are just going to try to live the best Christian life you can. You want be Christ like. Do not think just because you got baptized the old you won't creep up! That's why we work on it daily. It is a lifetime commitment.

Now I would like to explain to you what the Baptismal Ceremony consist of, therefore you will not be afraid. Always remember that God did not give you the spirit of fear.

2 Timothy 1:7

For God hath not given us the spirit of fear; but of power, and of love, and of a sound mind.

(Continued)

PREPARING FOR BAPTISM

The Baptismal Ceremony is this simple:

(I am sure every church or ceremony is different)

1. You are prayed for and asked some questions about your Savior JESUS CHRIST.

2. You get dressed in all white, including underclothes, T-shirts, a bathing cap (for women and little girls to protect their hair), and baptismal gowns.

3. You are escorted to the Sanctuary to line up, while beautiful music is playing.

4. You are escorted to the Baptismal Pool.

5. In the Baptismal Pool, there are normally two people. (One Pastor and one Deacon for Assistance) Remember I am sure every church or ceremony is different.

6. You are helped into the Baptismal Pool by another escort (Deacon).

(Continued)

PREPARING FOR BAPTISM

7. Once inside the Baptismal Pool, the Pastor or the assistant (Deacon) will tell you to hold your breath (you may also want to hold your nose), while placing his hand on your back for support and possibly the back of your head. The assisting Deacon will also be holding you with his hands for firm support. *(You are about to be baptized—relax you are God's child)*

8. You will hear the Preacher/Pastor say, "I baptize you in the name of the Father, the Son and the Holy Spirit."

9. Then they both will put you under the water quickly, about a second or two.

10. You will hear applause because we are proud of you.

11. Next, you are handed a towel and will be escorted out of the Baptismal Pool by an escort (Deacon).

Note: You may feel cold from the water, don't let that alarm you.

12. Now, you are BAPTIZED!
        CONGRATULATIONS PRAISE THE LORD!

(Continued)

PREPARING FOR BAPTISM

You are immediately received by a Deacon to change back into your dry clothes and then you return to the rest of the Baptismal Ceremony!

It is normally good to get baptized when you understand it and when you want to or feel the Holy Spirit telling you to. Never be forced to get baptized. Ask Questions!

It is best to get baptized before the age thirteen. Thirteen is the age when sins count on you but you can do it at any age, just don't be afraid.

This is dedicated to Joseph Allen Ashe, Sr. Congratulations on your recent baptism. My daughter MoNae Lewis, she was baptized on March 02, 2005. My mother and I were baptized a long time ago.

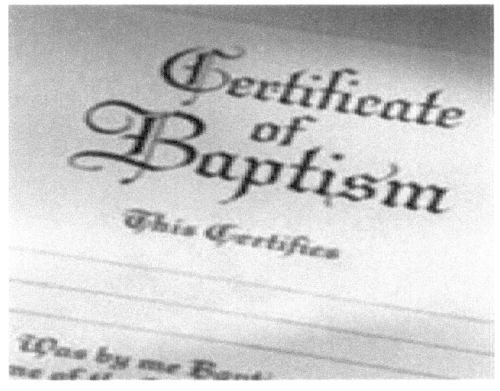

Matthew 3:11
Baptism signifies repentance.

USING MUSIC TO GET THROUGH

The emotions I feel are incredible, I love to Praise the Lord!
When the choir sings at church, we are on one Accord

If there was no spiritual music, I would not know what to do
It doesn't matter what song I hear,
It seems like God has ordered it to get me through!

I'm so grateful for Gospel music,
Because when I cannot hear the Word of God or write poetry,

I turn on inspirational radio when I'm going through a situation
Or put on a Gospel CD…
BECAUSE MUSIC LIFTS MY SPIRITS AND MINISTERS TO ME!

Exodus 15:1

Music can be used to worship God.

I AM SOMEBODY TOO

I know I look different and down on my luck,
I haven't eaten in days, I'm in a rut

My hot water has been turned off, my electric too,
My gas is next and I don't know what to do!

I have small children and one on the way
As soon as I gave my husband the good news,
He left me that very day

He said, "He loved me but can't take the pressures of life."
Yes, you heard me, he left his wife!

I started to feel bad and blame myself for this mess
Then I heard God's Voice say, "You are not anything less,
Just because you don't have as much as you had before
You never stop calling for Me daily and praying more."

God said, "My child, don't give up or lose hope,
Because I will take care of you

(Continued)

I AM SOMEBODY TOO

Now, go stand and look into the mirror;
And repeat out loud,
I AM SOMEBODY TOO!"

Now I can go to sleep tonight and be in perfect peace

I don't worry about tomorrow because,
GOD WILL NEVER ABANDON ME!"

Isaiah 26:3

He will keep you in perfect peach whose mind is stayed on Him.

TSUNAMI/HURRICANE KATRINA

Tsunami/Hurricane Katrina Tragedy

The Tsunami and Hurricane Katrina came,
And their land and state was devastated

The devastation and suffering was everywhere you looked;
The world watched and prayed as our hearts broke

It was so sad to see what is going on in their state and land,
I still had to remember that everything is a part of God's plan

Nevertheless, I am human therefore I felt their pain;
And I wondered what was the next step to do?

(Continued)

TSUNAMI/HURRICANE KATRINA

For now, I will pray for peace and future prosperity
As they re-build their lives back;
And send love from my heart to you

I thank God for you that are donating,
Or that is lending a helping hand
You are a blessing to these beautiful people,
Who yet don't understand

They don't understand why this happened to them so suddenly?
They are asking why did it have to happen to me?

Dear Hearts,
In life we will never know all the answers why,
We just pray to God and thank Him for another day

I am also praying that God blesses you and protect you,
In Jesus' name I Pray!

Psalm 9:9

The Lord also will be a refuge for the oppressed, a refuge in times of trouble.

I CAN'T FORGET

I CAN'T FORGET…
Jesus You were crucified on the Cross on Calvary,
And rose from the dead on day three

I CAN'T FORGET…
You died for all our sins and paid the price,
What a sacrifice!

I CAN'T FORGET…
To worship God for the rest of my days

I CAN'T FORGET…
Jesus You promised to return,
But it is Salvation first that we must earn

I CAN'T FORGET…
The simple rules to be saved

Just believe in your heart and confess with your mouth,
That Jesus is the Son of God and He died for our sins

(Continued)

I CANT FORGET

I CAN'T FORGET…

That Romans 10:9-10 is all you required to get IN

TO BE SAVED PRAY THIS PRAYER:

Heavenly Father, in the name of Jesus, I present myself to you. I pray and ask Jesus to be the Lord over my life. I believe it in my heart that Jesus has been raised from the dead. I will make Him the Lord over my life. Jesus, come into my heart. I believe that I am saved, reborn and a Christian. I am a child of Almighty God. In Jesus' name. Amen.

Romans 10:9-10

That if you confess with your mouth, "Jesus is Lord," and believe in your heart that God raised Him from the dead, you will be saved. For it is with your heart that you believe and are justified, and it is with your mouth that you confess and are saved.

JESUS IS MY FRIEND

Jesus is more than my Savior, He is my Friend
I can call on Him in midnight hour,
When no one else is up to care
He is awake listening, He is always there

He gives me advice even when I am asleep
I see Him in my dreams,
I hear His Voice like a calm rivers stream

Talking to my Friend gives me peace,
That everything is going to be alright
He also assures me that there is no battle,
He could not win or could not fight

I am very grateful for my Friend Jesus,
He is so awesome; I cannot keep it to myself!
My friend is always there when I have no one else

Accept Him in your life and He will be your Friend too
Just accept Him as Lord and Savior, it is simple to do

James 2:23
We can be Friends with God.

THE INVITATION

I WANT TO GIVE YOU AN INVITATION TO BE SAVED.

JOHN 3:16

FOR GOD SO LOVED THE WORLD HE GAVE HIS ONLY BEGOTTEN SON, SO WHOMEVER BELIEVES IN HIM SHALL NOT PERISH BUT HAVE ETERNAL LIFE.

THE INVITATION

I want to give you an Invitation to be SAVED:

PRAY WITH A SINCERE HEART:

God, I accept Jesus Christ as my Savior. I ask you to come into my life, I repent for all my sins and believe that Jesus Christ is Lord and I believe He rose from the dead on the third day with all power in His Hands. I want to serve you with my whole heart from this day forward. I will try to live the best Christian life and put you first in everything I do. In Jesus' name I pray. Amen.

OR PRAY YOUR OWN SINCERE PRAYER.

Now, Read the Scriptures below:

(If you have done this you are now SAVED)

John 3:16

For God so loved the world that He gave His only begotten Son, that whoever believes in Him should not perish but have everlasting life.

ALSO, READ ROMANS 10:9-10 AGAIN!

WHERE ARE YOU GOING?

Give your life to Jesus Christ Today!

AND GET SAVED

Call me Toll Free 1-877-782-5550

And talk to ME!

I MINISTER TO SOULS FOR THE KINGDOM!

Anelda Ballard aka Jazzy Kitty

INSPIRATIONAL SCRIPTURES
OLD TESTAMENT:

GENESIS 28:15, NKJV Behold, I *am* with you and will keep you wherever you go, and will bring you back to this land; for I will not leave you until I have done what I have spoken to you."

PSALM 18:2, KJV The Lord is my rock, and my fortress, and my deliverer; my God, my strength, in whom I will trust...the horn of my salvation, and my high tower.

PSALM 27:14, NKJV Wait on the Lord; Be of good courage, And He shall strengthen your heart; Wait, I say, on the LORD.

PSALM 46:1, KJV God is our refuge and strength, a very pleasant help in trouble.

PSALM 55:22, NKJV Cast your burden on the Lord, and He shall sustain you; He shall never permit the righteous to be moved.

PSALM 100:4, KJV Enter into His gates with thanksgiving, and into His courts with praise: be thankful unto Him, and bless His name.

OLD TESTAMENT:

PSALM 147:3, NKJV He heals the brokenhearted, and binds up their wounds.

PROVERBS 1:23, KJV Behold, I pour out my spirit unto you, I will make known my words unto you.

PROVERBS 3:5-6, NKJV Trust in the Lord with all your heart, and lean not on your own understanding; In all your ways acknowledge Him, and He shall direct your paths.

PROVERBS 12:2, NIV A good man obtains favor from the Lord, but the Lord condemns a crafty man.

ISAIAH 54:17, NKJV No weapon formed against you shall prosper, and every tongue which rises against you in judgment you shall condemn. This is the heritage of the servants of the Lord, and their righteousness is from Me.

JEREMIAH 17:7, NKJV Blessed is the man who trust in the Lord, and whose hope in the Lord.

NEW TESTAMENT:

MATTHEW 6:33, NKJV But seek first the Kingdom of God and His righteousness, and all these things shall be added to you.

MATTHEW 9:13, NKJV But go and learn what *this* means: *'I desire mercy and not sacrifice'* For I did not come to call the righteous, but sinners, to repentance."

MATTHEW 11:28, NKJV Come to Me, all you who labor and are heavy laden, and I will give you rest.

MATTHEW 21:22, KJV And all things, whatsoever ye shall ask in prayer, believing, ye shall receive.

LUKE 1:37, NLT For nothing is impossible with God.

LUKE 6:38, KJV Give, and it shall be given unto you; good measure, pressed down, and shaken together, and running over, shall men give into your bosom...For with the same measure that ye mete withal it shall be measured to you again.

LUKE 18:20, NIV You know the commandments: 'Do not commit adultery, do not murder, do not steal, do not give false testimony, honor thy father and mother.'

NEW TESTAMENT:

LUKE 23:34, NKJV Then said Jesus, "Father, forgive them; for they know not what they do." And they divided His garments and cast lots.

JOHN 4:12, KJV God is a Spirit: and they that worship Him must worship Him in spirit and truth.

John 5:24, NKJV He who hears My word and believes in Him who sent Me has everlasting life, and shall not come into judgment, but has passed from death to life.

John 6:35, KJV And Jesus said unto them, "I am the bread of life: he that cometh to me shall never hunger; and he that believeth on me shall never thirst."

John 14:1, KJV Let not your heart be troubled: ye believe in God, believe also in Me.

John 14:2-3, KJV In my Father's house are many mansions: if it were not so, I would have told you. I go to prepare a place for you. And if I go and prepare a place for you, I will come again.

John 14:14, NLT Yes, ask anything in my name, and I will do it!

NEW TESTAMENT:

Romans 6:23, KJV For the wages of sin is death; but the gift of God is eternal life through Jesus Christ our Lord.

Romans 8:35, 37 KJV Who shall separate us from the love of Christ? Shall tribulation, or distress, or persecution, or famine, or nakedness, or peril, or sword? Nay, in all these things we are more that conquerors through Him that loved us.

1 Corinthians 2:9, KJV But it is written, Eye hath not seen, nor ear heard, neither have entered into the heart of man, the things which God hath prepared for them that love Him.

2 Corinthians 5:7, KJV For we walk by faith, not by sight.

2 Corinthians 5:17, KJV Therefore if any man be in Christ, He is a new creature: old things are passed away; behold, all things are become new.

Ephesians 2:8, NIV For by grace are ye saved through faith; and that not of yourselves it is the gift of God.

Philippians 4:13, NKJV I can do all things through Christ who strengthens me.

NEW TESTAMENT:

2 Timothy 1:7, KJV For God hath not given us the spirit of fear, but of power, and of love, and of a sound mind.

2 Timothy 2:15, NIV Do your best to present yourself to God as one is approved, a workman who does not need to be ashamed and who correctly handles the word of truth.

Hebrews 10:23, KJV Let us hold fast the profession of our faith without wavering; (for He is faithful that promised).

Hebrews 11:1, NIV Now Faith is the substance of things hoped for, the evidence of things not seen.

Hebrews 11:6, KJV But without faith it is impossible to please Him: for he that cometh to God must believe that He is, and that He is a rewarder of them that diligently seek Him.

James 1:5, NKJV If any of you lacks wisdom, let him ask of God, who gives to all liberally and without reproach, and it will be given to him.

1 Peter 5:7, NLT Give all your worries and cares to God, for He cares about you.

NEW TESTAMENT:

2 Peter 3:9, NKJV The Lord is not slack concerning His promise, as some count slackness, but is longsuffering toward us, not willing that any should perish but that all should come to repentance.

1 John 1:9, KJV If we confess our sins, He is faithful and just to forgive us our sins, and to cleanse us from all unrighteousness.

1 John 4:19, KJV We love Him, because He first loved us.

Revelation 3:20, KJV Behold I stand at the door, and knock: if any man hear my voice, and open the door; I will come in to him, and will sup with him, and he with Me.

CLOSING PRAYER

Heavenly Father,

We say Thank you once again
Now that this assignment from You has come to an end
I, your servant, pray from my heart that this book will
Bless lives the way it has blessed my mother and I from the start

Heavenly Father, in addition,
I am also asking for a special blessing for everyone in the world,
Especially for all the people that is hurting in any way

Most importantly, Father
I pray that the world accepts Your precious Son Jesus Christ who
Is my mother's and I personal Savior

Lord, if this book touches just one soul or life then
Our purpose is done

Heavenly Father, I want everyone to feel the same love
For You and for Your Son and prayerfully have the same
Relationship as we do

In Jesus' name I pray. Amen

Ephesians 6:18
Pray all the time.

ASSIGNMENT COMPLETED

POETRY IS OUR MINISTRY

TO GOD BE THE GLORY!

www.ingramcontent.com/pod-product-compliance
Lightning Source LLC
Chambersburg PA
CBHW031256290426
44109CB00012B/613